Eco-Innovations

Eco-Innovations

Freya Storm

CONTENTS

Introduction	1
1 Benefits of Eco-Innovations	3
2 Sustainable Energy Solutions	5
3 Green Transportation Technologies	7
4 Smart Agriculture and Food Production	10
5 Waste Management and Recycling	13
6 Water Conservation Technologies	16
7 Eco-Friendly Building and Construction	19
8 Sustainable Fashion and Textiles	22
9 Renewable Materials and Packaging	25
10 Environmental Monitoring and Data Analysis	28
11 Green Electronics and E-Waste Management	31
12 Eco-Tourism and Sustainable Travel	34
13 Education and Awareness for Sustainability	37

14 Government Policies and Regulations 40

Conclusion 43

Enjoyed This Book? Let Others Know! 45

Copyright © 2025 by Freya Storm

All rights reserved. No part of this book may be reproduced in any manner whatsoever without written permission except in the case of brief quotations embodied in critical articles and reviews.

First Printing, 2025

Introduction

The development of technology has been a cornerstone of economic and social progress throughout history. It has revolutionized the production of goods and services, enabling efficiency and reducing cost structures. Innovations in public transportation and infrastructure have continually transformed urban landscapes, driving the success of economies of scale. Simultaneously, advancements in communication technologies have significantly reduced spatial barriers, fostering unprecedented levels of economic integration and enhancing political transparency.

This relentless drive toward economic efficiency has propelled humanity to achieve remarkable technological breakthroughs. These advancements not only reinforce the benefits of economies of scale but also further dissolve spatial limitations, allowing for more seamless global connectivity. In essence, innovation emerges as an inevitable by-product of economic development, a self-reinforcing cycle where technological progress catalyzes growth and vice versa. Historically, the correlation between technological advancement and economic growth is undeniable. For instance, during the Industrial Revolution in the United Kingdom—a period marked by rapid technological progress—the rate of per capita income growth from 1800 to 1870 far surpassed that of any previous era.

The argument in this book aligns with this perspective: faced with pressing global crises and limited policy solutions, the pursuit of transformative technological innovation may serve as the "miracle cure" needed to counter destructive growth patterns.

Technology has already woven itself into the fabric of our daily lives, influencing and reshaping how we live, work, and interact. From consumer devices designed to enhance convenience and flexibility to advances in e-commerce that provide seamless shopping experiences, technology continues to evolve. Social media platforms bridge geographical divides, reconnecting individuals who might have otherwise drifted apart. Scientific research produces groundbreaking solutions to complex medical challenges. Transportation technologies make movement more accessible and efficient, while advancements in manufacturing elevate productivity to unprecedented levels. The ripple effects of technological progress touch nearly every facet of modern existence, paving the way for a more interconnected and innovative future.

1

Benefits of Eco-Innovations

Eco-innovations present undeniable advantages that are not only compelling in theory but are also essential in practice. These innovations are pivotal in reducing negative environmental impacts while offering practical solutions for sustainability. For example, green processing techniques, environmentally friendly vehicles, and sustainable packaging solutions significantly minimize waste and energy consumption, contributing to a healthier planet.

Moreover, eco-innovations often lead to substantial cost savings. Green processing, for instance, utilizes fewer energy resources and natural inputs, resulting in reduced fuel and supply chain expenses. These financial benefits extend beyond operational efficiencies; they enhance a company's reputation in an increasingly eco-conscious marketplace. Modern consumers display a strong preference for environmentally friendly and socially responsible brands—a trend that has intensified over recent years. Businesses adopting eco-innovations can capitalize on this shift in consumer behavior, gaining favor, mitigating risks, and securing long-term success.

This eco-conscious movement exemplifies the synergy between technology and environmentalism, fostering a new wave of eco-innovations. Defined as products and processes that positively impact the environment during their production, usage, or disposal, eco-innovations are emerging as vital tools in the fight against climate change. Many climate scientists underscore that significant reductions in greenhouse gas emissions will only be achievable through the widespread adoption of such technologies. Consequently, the development of eco-innovations has become a critical priority for ensuring the sustainability of our planet.

The focus of eco-innovation typically revolves around two key drivers: technological advancement and consumer behavior. Companies play an instrumental role by providing solutions that help consumers reduce their ecological footprint. From energy-efficient appliances to waste-reducing manufacturing methods, these innovations empower individuals and industries to tread more lightly on the planet. As climate scientists emphasize, prioritizing the adoption and development of eco-innovations is essential for achieving meaningful environmental progress.

Despite their promise, the journey of eco-innovation is not without challenges. Technical, financial, and policy-related obstacles often hinder the pace of development. Overcoming these hurdles requires coordinated efforts from governments, businesses, and consumers, all working collectively to embrace sustainable practices and invest in a greener future.

2

Sustainable Energy Solutions

The year 2020 revealed an important truth: factors beyond the control of technology—such as the devastating impact of a global pandemic—are among the few occurrences capable of delivering a meaningful short-term reduction in global carbon emissions. This realization shed light on the deep interconnectedness of energy consumption and carbon emissions. It underscored the fact that addressing emissions at their core requires a fundamental shift in how we power our world. A lasting solution demands an almost complete reliance on renewable energy sources to meet the global demand for electricity.

This need for clean, sustainable electricity cannot be overstated. Electricity alone accounts for 42% of global energy usage and contributes to approximately 37% of $CO2$ emissions. Yet, despite its critical role in reducing emissions, renewable energy—dominated by solar and wind power—currently occupies only a modest portion of the 27% renewable energy share. The primary bottleneck has been the lack of mature, efficient, and scalable energy storage technologies. Fortunately, emerging technologies are beginning to bridge this gap, enabling improvements in energy efficiency and generating renewable energy more cost-effectively without requiring extensive storage solutions. These advancements are capturing global attention as they hold the potential to transform our energy landscape.

The COVID-19 pandemic, while causing profound and far-reaching changes in all aspects of life, also highlighted the urgency of decarbonization in achieving sustainable energy solutions. The virus took an unprecedented toll, claiming over two million lives globally, yet it also brought about a measurable reduction in carbon emissions. The International Energy Agency (IEA) projected a 7% global decline in energy-related CO2 emissions for 2020—a level not seen in a decade. While this temporary reduction reflected the scale of the economic slowdown rather than a systemic shift, it served as a sobering reminder of the urgency of pursuing genuine and lasting solutions.

However, these reductions are no cause for celebration. Instead, what we should acknowledge is the opportunity this period has provided: a chance to accelerate the adoption of innovative technologies that, when applied and scaled effectively, can consistently reduce emissions to net zero. These advancements sow the seeds of decarbonization, building the foundation for a sustainable energy future.

The road ahead is challenging, but the potential for transformative change is immense. Sustainable energy solutions are not just about mitigating climate change; they represent an opportunity to rethink and rebuild the systems that power our world. With the right investments, policies, and technological breakthroughs, a cleaner and more resilient energy future is within reach.

3

Green Transportation Technologies

Green transportation technologies have emerged as vital tools in reducing transport-related carbon emissions, offering promising alternatives that are less harmful to the environment. A comprehensive analysis of Green IT identifies four primary technological innovations with the potential to significantly cut emissions within a structured timeframe.

1. Smart Logistics Planning and Real-Time Management The first approach involves leveraging smart logistics systems to optimize transportation efficiency. By integrating real-time navigational data with existing topographical information, these systems enable drivers to avoid obstacles and select the most efficient routes. This reduces fuel consumption and travel time, while minimizing overall carbon emissions. The seamless combination of real-time data and predictive analytics transforms logistics planning into a more sustainable process.

2. Intelligent Eco-Driving The second innovation focuses on intelligent eco-driving systems, which estimate and optimize traffic speed based on real-time data. By incorporating a topographical database that reflects live traffic speeds and conditions, these systems can guide vehicles to achieve optimal fuel efficiency. Additionally, advanced mathematical models are being developed to account for factors such as fuel consumption, travel time, road grades, vehicle characteristics, and variable speed limits. These insights help design solutions that improve energy efficiency while reducing environmental impact. Though fully electric vehicles may currently face limitations in achieving interstate speeds, they serve as a crucial step in replacing traditional gasoline-powered cars.

3. Future Vehicle Technologies The third area emphasizes the development of next-generation vehicle technologies, including electric and hydrogen fuel cell vehicles. These innovations hold immense potential for efficiency and sustainability, paving the way for a cleaner future. With advancements in battery technology and renewable energy integration, electric vehicles are becoming increasingly practical and accessible. Similarly, hydrogen fuel cell vehicles promise zero emissions and high efficiency, presenting an attractive alternative for long-distance and commercial transportation.

4. Smart Urban Environments Finally, smart urban environment concepts are being designed to tackle challenges such as traffic congestion, noise pollution, and urban carbon emissions. These initiatives involve creating intelligent transportation systems that prioritize public transit, improve traffic flow, and promote alternative mobility options like cycling and walking. By integrating technology and urban planning, these concepts aim to make cities more livable and environmentally friendly.

Beyond technological advancements, several key factors drive the shift toward green transportation. Geophysical and environmental considerations, government policies, shifting consumer behaviors, and awareness of human impact on the environment all contribute to the pursuit of zero CO_2 emissions. Transportation, which has become one of the largest contributors to greenhouse gas emissions, poses a critical challenge in the journey toward sustainability.

| 9 | – GREEN TRANSPORTATION TECHNOLOGIES

Over recent decades, the share of emissions attributable to transportation has grown significantly, coinciding with an increase in global logistics demands. This has created an urgent need for innovative green technologies to neutralize emissions and address the transportation crisis. Comprehensive research and monitoring efforts are essential in identifying the core technologies and strategic priorities necessary for sustainable transportation development.

This analysis ultimately highlights the importance of selecting priority areas for implementing Green IT solutions. By aligning these solutions with global sustainability goals, we can accelerate the transition to low-emission transportation systems that meet the demands of a modern, interconnected world.

4

Smart Agriculture and Food Production

Innovative solutions in smart agriculture and food production are transforming how we grow, manage, and sustain food resources. These technologies bridge the gap between traditional farming practices and modern demands for efficiency, sustainability, and environmental responsibility.

1. CropX: Precision Soil Monitoring CropX is a pioneering company that has introduced wafer-sized sensors designed to be distributed across fields at strategic intervals. These advanced sensors continuously collect critical data on soil moisture levels, temperature, and humidity. The CropX app processes this data, providing farmers with actionable insights to optimize irrigation, improve crop yields, and reduce resource waste. By leveraging such precision tools, CropX exemplifies the transformative potential of technology in agriculture.

2. Eco-Farm: Biodegradable Nanotechnology Eco-Farm is at the forefront of natural pesticide solutions, utilizing nanoparticles to revolutionize agricultural practices. Their main innovation lies in the development of 100% biodegradable nanofiber carriers, designed to enhance the efficacy of pesticides without causing harm to soil or plants. These carriers improve the targeted action rate of insecticidal agents, reducing the environmental footprint of pest control. Currently, two insecticidal drugs are being integrated into Eco-Farm carriers, showcasing the company's commitment to sustainability and innovation.

3. DECLARE: Prolonging Food Shelf Life DECLARE, a Chinese company, has developed innovative food storage bags made from a special wax-infused material. These DECLARE bags have the remarkable ability to extend the shelf life of food up to a thousand-fold, addressing one of the most pressing issues in global food waste. The company is actively raising investments through crowdfunding platforms like Indiegogo, signaling a growing interest in scalable solutions for food preservation.

4. Biobak: Enhancing Soil Health Biobak is dedicated to enriching artificial soil carbon content by acting as an accelerant for bacterial activity. The bacterial food source utilized by Biobak is derived from waste products of industries with partial vegetal origins. The company claims that its technology can increase soil carbonic compound content more than thirtyfold, providing a significant boost to soil fertility and productivity. Such innovations highlight the role of biological solutions in sustainable farming.

Smart Agriculture: Harnessing Data and Technology Despite the challenges posed by global food security, the integration of advanced technology offers a clear path forward. Recognized by global entities like the United Nations and the World Economic Forum, the importance of utilizing high-tech solutions to safeguard harvests is undeniable. Until recently, farming tools consisted of rudimentary equipment like pencils, paper, and weather vanes. Today, however, smart agriculture—also known as precision agriculture—leverages vast pools of data to revolutionize farming practices.

The key segments of smart agriculture include specialized apps and software capable of storing and processing critical information.

These tools can forecast crop yields, predict diseases, determine optimal sowing periods, recommend suitable fertilizers, and calculate precise herbicide and pesticide dosages. With approximately 2,019 startups creating similar technologies—80% of which focus on terra technologies—the agriculture industry is experiencing a wave of innovation that promises to redefine efficiency and sustainability.

Alternative Food Sources: A Necessary Evolution In addition to advancements in agricultural practices, alternative food sources are gaining traction as viable solutions to global food challenges. These include innovations like lab-grown dry-aged meat, protein flours, and nutrient-dense products derived from seaweed, crickets, and ascidians. Such developments offer sustainable and environmentally friendly options for meeting the dietary needs of a growing population.

The intersection of smart agriculture and alternative food production represents a promising frontier in addressing the global food crisis. By embracing these technologies and strategies, humanity can create a more sustainable, resilient, and equitable food system for future generations.

5

Waste Management and Recycling

In the modern business landscape, effective systems for managing production waste have become essential. Many forward-thinking companies are leveraging innovative technologies to address this challenge, particularly in the consumer goods sector. These organizations are at the forefront of developing greener solutions, advancing the principles of a circular economy, and utilizing artificial intelligence (AI) to enhance waste management and recycling practices.

Circular Economy and Transforming Waste into Treasure
Effective waste management begins with state-managed strategies aimed at redefining waste as a valuable resource rather than a liability. These strategies align with the principles of the circular economy, which seeks to minimize waste by reusing, recycling, and recovering materials wherever possible. By transforming waste into treasure, these efforts not only reduce environmental impact but also create economic opportunities. Zero-waste initiatives and circular economy hubs are being implemented worldwide, demonstrating their potential to generate sustainable economic growth while minimizing ecological harm.

The Role of Technology in Waste Management Advanced technologies play a critical role in enhancing waste management systems. For example, AI-driven solutions can optimize sorting processes, identify recyclable materials more efficiently, and reduce contamination in recycling streams. These technologies enable companies to innovate and adapt, ensuring that waste is managed sustainably and cost-effectively. By embracing these advancements, businesses can align their operations with environmental goals while maintaining competitive advantages in an increasingly eco-conscious market.

Eco-Packaging: A Shift Toward Sustainability One significant area of focus in waste management is packaging. Often, companies invest as much in the development of their packaging as they do in the products themselves. This is because packaging serves multiple functions, from protecting goods to enhancing their appeal. However, traditional packaging materials often contribute to significant waste and environmental degradation.

Eco-packaging, while a relatively new concept, is rapidly gaining traction. This "back to nature" approach seeks to minimize the environmental footprint of packaging by using sustainable, biodegradable, and recyclable materials. It shifts the focus from products as the central component of the ecological equation to the entire lifecycle of the materials used. With growing consumer awareness and demand for greener packaging solutions, companies are increasingly adopting these innovations, moving closer to a sustainable future.

Challenges and Opportunities While significant progress has been made, challenges persist. Many businesses continue to rely on older technologies, reluctant to abandon them as long as they remain functional. This hesitation can slow the adoption of newer, more sustainable practices. However, the global push for sustainability, coupled with advancements in technology, presents a unique opportunity to drive transformative change.

Waste management and recycling are no longer just environmental imperatives—they are strategic priorities for creating value in a resource-constrained world. By combining innovative technologies, state-managed strategies, and a commitment to sustainability, businesses and governments can pave the way for a cleaner, more efficient, and economically vibrant future.

6

Water Conservation Technologies

Water conservation has become an increasingly critical priority in the face of growing water scarcity and rising ecological concerns. Innovative technologies are stepping up to address this challenge, offering practical solutions that empower households and industries to reduce water consumption effectively.

1. Eco-Friendly Dishwashers: Revolutionizing Water Efficiency One significant advancement in water conservation is the development of eco-friendly dishwashers. These appliances are designed to minimize water usage by recirculating water from the pre-rinse stage for reuse in the main dishwashing cycle. This innovative approach drastically reduces the amount of water a household consumes daily. Additionally, these dishwashers operate efficiently without relying on extremely hot water, further conserving energy and reducing demand on hot water heaters. The resulting non-heat-generated water savings can reach up to 60% compared to traditional handwashing practices.

Modern eco-friendly dishwashers offer advanced features that place control directly in the hands of users. For instance, many models allow customization of water settings, enabling users to minimize consumption while still achieving sparkling-clean dishes. As consumer demand for sustainable appliances grows, manufacturers worldwide have adopted stringent standards to enhance water efficiency in their designs.

2. The Role of Municipal Regulations in Water Conservation While many households may be unaware of municipal restrictions on water usage, these regulations are becoming increasingly common, especially during hot summer months. Penalties for exceeding water limits can serve as a powerful incentive to adopt conservation measures. For example, a 3% penalty on overuse, combined with steep markups, can quickly highlight the financial benefits of investing in water-saving technologies.

3. Technological Innovations in Water Conservation The rise of eco-consciousness has spurred significant advancements in water conservation technologies, many of which empower households to monitor and manage their water consumption with greater precision. From smart faucets to irrigation systems that adjust water flow based on weather patterns, these innovations put more control in the hands of consumers.

Eco-friendly appliances, like advanced dishwashers, have set a high bar for water-saving capabilities. These technologies not only contribute to environmental preservation but also offer tangible financial benefits by reducing utility bills. As a result, they exemplify the growing sophistication of water conservation efforts in modern households.

4. Shaping a Water-Conscious Future The evolution of water conservation technologies represents a significant shift in how we view and manage our most precious resource. By adopting eco-friendly solutions and adhering to stricter efficiency standards, households and industries alike can play a vital role in addressing water scarcity challenges. The combination of technological innovation, regulatory measures, and growing consumer awareness is paving the way for a more sustainable and water-conscious future.

7

Eco-Friendly Building and Construction

Sustainable construction is at the forefront of modern innovation, offering solutions to reduce the environmental impact of building practices. Among these solutions, 3D printing technology has emerged as a game-changer, particularly for creating space habitats and eco-friendly structures.

1. 3D Printing: Revolutionizing Construction 3D printing is a transformative approach that significantly reduces the resources, time, and human labor required in construction. In the case of space habitats, the process primarily involves using materials in the form of slabs that are later assembled into walls. This streamlined method requires only five essential components for manufacturing: removable slabs, bases for their bonds from previous printing stages, bonding matrices, reels for deploying pipes with locally produced internals, and protective shells to shield cables from Local Environmental Systems (LES). By minimizing material delivery needs and reducing waste, 3D printing embodies the principles of sustainability and efficiency.

2. The Challenges of Traditional Construction Traditional building practices face significant sustainability challenges, particularly due to the transportation of materials. Before construction even begins, the delivery of industrial equipment, metal products, and cement creates a considerable carbon footprint. During the building phase, additional materials such as reinforcement bars, formwork supplies, and finishing materials—including paint, countertops, drywall, and electrical equipment—are transported, further amplifying energy consumption.

The inefficiency of traditional construction extends to the finished product. Spaces designed for living often become occupied by cabinets, shelves, and other elements that detract from their functionality and energy efficiency. This highlights the need for innovative solutions that prioritize resource conservation and sustainable design.

3. The Promise of Eco-Friendly Innovations Eco-friendly construction technologies, such as 3D printing, address many of these challenges by reducing the reliance on transported materials and minimizing waste. By enabling localized production and efficient assembly, these technologies align with global sustainability goals. Beyond resource efficiency, eco-friendly innovations offer the potential to reimagine how buildings are designed, constructed, and utilized.

4. Toward a Sustainable Future in Construction The evolution of eco-friendly building and construction practices represents a critical step in mitigating the environmental impact of urban development. By adopting advanced technologies like 3D printing, the construction industry can reduce its carbon footprint, conserve resources, and create structures that are both functional and sustainable.

The integration of these innovations into mainstream practices requires collaboration between researchers, engineers, policymakers, and industry leaders. With continued investment and innovation, eco-friendly construction technologies have the potential to transform not just how we build but also how we envision the spaces we inhabit.

8

Sustainable Fashion and Textiles

Sustainable fashion is a cutting-edge intersection of design, technology, and environmental responsibility, and few exemplify this better than textile pioneer Suzanne Lee. Her groundbreaking works merge biological materials with creative couture, showcasing the extraordinary possibilities of eco-conscious innovation in the fashion industry.

1. Suzanne Lee: Redefining Fashion with Biology Suzanne Lee's recent designs bring organic materials like plants and apples into the realm of fashion. Her earlier works, such as dresses combining leather discs with vegetable fibers and hemp pants paired with uniquely crafted stockings, highlight her innovative approach to integrating natural elements into clothing. Additionally, her collaborations with other designers utilize materials that originate in scientific laboratories, blending functionality with artistic expression.

Lee's creations embrace the fragility and uniqueness of organic materials, which are often challenging to handle. As a result, her garments are frequently exhibited using tailor's forms, creating visually stunning displays that celebrate the symbiosis of biology and the body. These displays capture a "time-recorded lived moment of biological technology," highlighting the transient nature of organic fashion and its potential to coalesce with our rapidly changing world. Lee's work speaks to her vision of fashion existing harmoniously within what she calls "transient landfills," reflecting both its temporary beauty and its sustainable legacy.

2. The Concept of Bio-Couture Suzanne Lee's revolutionary concept of "bio-couture" pushes the boundaries of traditional textile production by integrating biological technology. Her vision involves growing fashion from bacteria, much like cultivating plants or farm animals, and creating garments that are entirely biodegradable. Using household bacteria and yeasts as key components, Lee has developed a process that fosters a symbiotic relationship between fabric fibers and nutrients.

The result is an innovative and sustainable approach to fashion manufacturing: threads are grown from cells, producing textiles as natural as they are functional. These garments require no soap to clean and leave no waste behind—ushering in a future where clothing maintenance and cultivation become seamless, eco-friendly processes.

3. The Role of Synthetic Biology in Fashion By combining synthetic biology tools with textile and apparel technologies, bio-couture enables a harmonious relationship between biology and design. This approach has the potential to revolutionize the industry, creating garments that are not only beautiful but also completely sustainable. Lee's work exemplifies how merging science and design can lead to a paradigm shift in how we think about clothing—turning fashion into a living, breathing entity that evolves alongside our environmental needs.

4. Expanding the Possibilities of Sustainable Textiles Imagine a fashion industry where threads are grown in laboratories, mimicking nature's processes, and garments are created with zero waste. Lee's vision sets the stage for an era where sustainability is embedded into every stage of the production cycle. Beyond fashion, this innovation offers solutions for reducing textile waste and mitigating the environmental impact of traditional manufacturing methods.

Sustainable fashion is more than a trend—it is a movement toward rethinking how materials are sourced, produced, and disposed of. The integration of biological technology into textiles brings us closer to a world where style and sustainability coexist effortlessly.

9

Renewable Materials and Packaging

The pervasive use of plastic in modern life poses one of the most significant challenges to environmental sustainability. Conventional plastics, primarily made from petrochemicals, are notoriously difficult to recycle due to a lack of standardized processes and inadequate infrastructure. In the United States, only 30% of plastic waste is recycled, compared to 63% in Europe—a stark disparity that highlights the need for more effective recycling systems. However, the rise of renewable materials and innovative packaging solutions offers a path forward in addressing this pressing issue.

1. Biodegradable Plastics: An Eco-Friendly Alternative
Biodegradable plastics represent a crucial step toward reducing the environmental impact of traditional plastic waste. Unlike conventional plastics, which take between 20 to 1,000 years to decompose, biodegradable plastics can break down within 3 to 6 months. This rapid decomposition is facilitated by microorganisms that consume the material, turning it into water, carbon dioxide, and biomass without releasing harmful greenhouse gases.

The environmental benefits of biodegradable plastics are substantial. By providing a sustainable solution that minimizes long-term waste accumulation, they offer a viable alternative for packaging and other plastic applications. Additionally, these materials help mitigate the harmful effects of conventional plastic decomposition, which contributes to greenhouse gas emissions and environmental pollution.

2. Bioplastics: The Power of Natural Materials Bioplastics take sustainability a step further by utilizing natural resources such as algae, yeast, and corn starch as their primary raw materials. These renewable inputs make bioplastics an eco-friendly alternative to traditional plastics, which are derived from toxic chemicals like benzene, toluene, and xylene—substances known to cause serious health issues, including cancer and birth defects.

One of the most innovative examples of bioplastics is mycelium-based material. Derived from fungi and agricultural waste, mycelium offers an organic, biodegradable solution for packaging and other applications. Not only can mycelium-based plastics be composted, but they can also be safely returned to the earth, where they enrich the soil instead of polluting it. This dual functionality underscores the potential of bioplastics to redefine sustainability in packaging.

3. Challenges and Opportunities in Renewable Packaging Despite their promise, renewable materials face challenges in scalability and consumer adoption. The infrastructure required to process and compost biodegradable and bioplastic materials is still developing, and widespread use will depend on global collaboration between governments, businesses, and researchers. However, as awareness of environmental issues grows, so does the demand for greener packaging solutions.

Renewable materials are not just about reducing waste—they also represent a shift toward circular economy practices that prioritize resource efficiency and material reuse. By investing in renewable packaging technologies, industries can reduce their ecological footprint while meeting the expectations of eco-conscious consumers.

4. Toward a Plastic-Free Future Plastic is deeply ingrained in our daily lives, making the transition to sustainable alternatives both challenging and essential. By embracing biodegradable plastics, bioplastics, and other renewable materials, we can take meaningful steps toward reducing the environmental impact of packaging and other plastic-based products. These innovations hold the key to a future where packaging is no longer synonymous with waste but instead serves as a symbol of sustainability and environmental stewardship.

10

Environmental Monitoring and Data Analysis

Environmental monitoring and data analysis play a critical role in addressing global ecological challenges and shaping effective policies. By leveraging high-quality environmental data, organizations like the European Environment Agency (EEA) are able to provide detailed, up-to-date insights on various environmental aspects. These efforts support the European Union (EU) and its member countries in developing informed and impactful policies for sustainable growth.

1. The Need for Innovative Monitoring Approaches Traditional environmental monitoring methods often demand significant resources and may fall short of meeting the comprehensive assessment needs of modern decision-making. This gap highlights the necessity of developing innovative monitoring approaches that prioritize efficiency, scalability, and accessibility for multiple users. To this end, the EEA's primary goal is to establish an efficient system that integrates advanced technologies and cost-effective methodologies.

One promising avenue is the adoption of **Key Access Technologies (KAT)**, which combine knowledge acquisition, technological transfer, and best practices into a unified framework. This approach involves deploying dispersed and localized monitoring platforms that collect, process, and analyze environmental data in real-time. By utilizing KAT, the EEA aims to create a robust monitoring infrastructure that supports diverse stakeholders, from policymakers to researchers and the general public.

2. The Importance of Monitoring for Policy and Knowledge Effective environmental monitoring is essential for managing ecosystems, shaping policy decisions, and expanding public understanding of environmental issues. The EEA recognizes the critical role of innovative technologies in achieving accurate and relevant environmental assessments. By adopting modern tools and methodologies, the agency can ensure that its findings are comprehensive and actionable.

Accurate environmental data also serve as a foundation for impactful communication. The EEA dedicates significant resources and expertise to keeping both experts and the public informed about the state of the environment. By translating complex data into clear, meaningful insights, the agency empowers decision-makers to address pressing ecological challenges and create policies with measurable social and political impact.

3. The Role of Advanced Technologies The integration of advanced technologies into environmental monitoring systems is revolutionizing how data is collected, analyzed, and applied. Tools such as remote sensing, satellite imaging, and IoT-enabled sensors provide real-time, high-resolution data on critical environmental indicators, including air and water quality, biodiversity, and climate patterns. These technologies enable the EEA to identify emerging trends, assess the effectiveness of interventions, and adapt strategies in response to dynamic ecological conditions.

Moreover, the use of data analytics, machine learning, and artificial intelligence enhances the agency's ability to process large datasets, uncover hidden patterns, and generate predictive models. By combining these technologies with traditional monitoring methods, the EEA can deliver insights that are both precise and actionable.

4. Creating Social and Political Impact Beyond technical advancements, the EEA is committed to fostering social and political change through its environmental monitoring efforts. By improving technologies and communication strategies, the agency can bridge the gap between scientific findings and public awareness. This, in turn, strengthens the connection between environmental knowledge and policy-making, ensuring that decisions are informed by the best available evidence.

Environmental monitoring and data analysis are not just about understanding the present—they are about shaping a sustainable future. Through innovation and collaboration, the EEA is laying the groundwork for a more resilient and informed global community.

11

Green Electronics and E-Waste Management

The growing challenge of electronic waste—commonly referred to as Waste Electrical and Electronic Equipment (WEEE)—presents significant environmental and legislative issues globally. Between 2011 and 2016, the expected rise in electronic waste necessitated critical adjustments to both national and international policies. With the global demand for electronics showing no sign of slowing, innovative approaches to managing e-waste and adopting greener practices in the electronics industry are more urgent than ever.

1. Rising Demand and Its Implications In the developed world, the number of mobile phone calls and text messages has plateaued. However, in developing countries, rapid growth in communication technology has led to an increasing demand for mobile phones, base stations, and access networks. While these emerging markets represent opportunities for growth, they also bring new environmental challenges.

The deployment of mobile telephony in developing countries, often equipped with green 2G and 3G technologies, has had limited direct impact on emissions in the developed world, which is transitioning to more efficient LTE (4G) technologies. However, in these regions, the overlay of new networks on older ones has resulted in a substantial increase in energy consumption and emissions. This growth has delayed the point at which the mobile network industry can achieve meaningful carbon reductions globally. Unlimited mobile calls from developing regions, for instance, are expected to slightly delay the peak of global mobile phone CO_2 emissions.

2. Voluntary Commitments and Toxic Substances In March 2010, eleven major consumer electronics companies made a voluntary commitment to phase out the use of numerous toxic substances commonly found in electronic equipment, starting in 2015. This initiative reflects the industry's growing recognition of its environmental responsibilities. As part of this commitment, these companies also pledged to increase recycling rates for their products, addressing the lifecycle impact of electronics.

The reliance on developing countries as destinations for discarded electronics presents a major ethical and environmental concern. Many end-of-life consumer electronics are shipped to these regions for recycling or storage, often exposing local populations to hazardous materials. This practice has sparked international protests and led to the introduction of stricter regulations.

The toxic substances set to be phased out by 2020 under the terms of the Electroindustry Voluntary Agreement significantly exceed the restrictions currently mandated by the EU's Restriction of Hazardous Substances (RoHS) directive. Furthermore, the agreement explicitly incorporates "design for environment" principles, emphasizing the importance of creating products that are easier to recycle and less harmful to the environment throughout their lifecycle.

3. The Need for Sustainable Resource Use A 2008 report from the United Nations Environment Programme (UNEP) highlighted the global demand for consumer electronics and the associated toxic substances—demand that continues to grow exponentially. The report estimated that up to 100 million tons of primary resources are consumed annually to meet the needs of the electronics sector. This boom underscores the urgent need for sustainable solutions that address both resource consumption and end-of-life management.

4. Paving the Way for Green Electronics Green electronics and effective e-waste management are critical to mitigating the environmental impact of the technology sector. Key strategies include adopting cleaner materials, phasing out hazardous substances, and improving recycling infrastructure worldwide. The principles of circular economy—focusing on reuse, refurbishment, and recycling—must be integrated into every stage of the electronics lifecycle.

The industry also needs to prioritize research and development into eco-friendly technologies, such as modular designs that extend product lifespans, biodegradable components, and energy-efficient devices. By combining regulatory measures with voluntary commitments from manufacturers, the transition to sustainable electronics can be accelerated.

Green electronics is not just a necessity; it is an opportunity to rethink how we design, produce, and manage technology. Through collective effort and innovative thinking, we can reduce the environmental footprint of electronics while meeting the growing demands of a connected world.

12

Eco-Tourism and Sustainable Travel

Tourism and travel are industries of profound duality. On one hand, sustainable tourism offers tremendous potential to boost employment, stimulate economic growth, protect the environment, and foster development within local communities. On the other hand, unchecked expansion often results in resource depletion, destruction of ecosystems, and significant carbon footprints. With global tourism contributing an estimated 5% of total greenhouse gas emissions, the question arises: can we make tourism more respectful, sustainable, and green?

1. The Promise of Sustainable Tourism Sustainable tourism is emerging as a powerful tool to integrate environmental responsibility with enriching travel experiences. Ethical travel practices, eco-tourism, and mindful adventures can align the triple bottom lines—people, planet, and profit—to benefit both humanity and the natural world. Through meaningful journeys, travelers gain transformative life experiences while fostering kindness, compassion, and respect for diverse cultures and ecosystems.

Innovative technologies and data-driven empowerment are also reshaping the travel industry. Platforms now allow customers to voice opinions and influence sustainable services or responsible destination choices. These tools engage younger, eco-conscious consumers who are deeply involved in global issues, often leveraging social media and activist movements to demand accountability. As such, sustainable tourism represents a shift in perceptions, attitudes, and actions toward protecting human heritage and safeguarding the environment.

2. The Role of Community-Based Corporations Voluntourism and community-based initiatives play an essential role in sustainable tourism. By encouraging collaboration between travelers, local communities, and businesses, these initiatives support sustainable workplaces and foster grassroots economic development. The current generation of eco-travelers—particularly Generation Z—is leading the charge toward green and responsible travel. Their values are transforming the industry, promoting environmental action, and driving demand for sustainable tourism practices.

3. Embracing Pragmatism and Responsibility Gone are the days of indulgent luxury in travel. Climate change has become both an existential threat and an economic crisis, necessitating a pragmatic and empathetic approach to tourism. Living with responsible sustainability is no longer an option but an imperative. The interconnected goals of the United Nations' 2030 Agenda for Sustainable Development—the "five Ps" of People, Planet, Prosperity, Peace, and Partnership—offer a roadmap for creating a more equitable and resilient travel industry. With less than a decade to achieve these goals, every stakeholder has a role to play.

Businesses and individuals failing to act responsibly risk losing both money and reputation in an increasingly eco-aware marketplace. Disruptive clean technologies, sustainable innovations, and eco-brands hold the key to societal and economic transformation. By investing in these areas, the travel industry can revive the economy while addressing the urgent need to reduce carbon footprints and embrace sustainable living.

4. Building a Better Future Through Sustainable Travel
The future of travel hinges on our ability to transition to a low-carbon economy, adopt sustainable lifestyles, and cultivate respect for others and the planet. Science and technology offer solutions that can bridge the gap between ecological challenges and transformative opportunities. The brilliance of tomorrow depends on wise investments today—choices that prioritize green technologies, responsible tourism practices, and thoughtful resource management.

Sustainable travel is more than a movement; it is a commitment to leaving the world better than we found it. By balancing exploration with preservation, humanity can redefine the purpose of tourism, ensuring that future generations inherit a planet rich in culture, biodiversity, and opportunity.

13

Education and Awareness for Sustainability

Education and awareness are fundamental drivers of sustainability, particularly in the realm of eco-innovation. By fostering a culture of environmental consciousness among managers, employees, and designers, companies can enhance the effectiveness of policies that support sustainable practices. Training programs that integrate environmental awareness with innovative product design not only build knowledge but also drive actionable change. However, these educational initiatives must be tailored to the specific needs and contexts of each organization.

1. Context-Dependent Educational Needs The educational requirements of a company are strongly influenced by its stage in the eco-innovation journey. Companies can be broadly categorized based on their experience with green supply chain management:

- **Companies with little experience** in green supply chains should prioritize foundational training. This includes raising awareness about the importance of sustainability, exploring potential improvements, and equipping staff with the tools and knowledge to implement basic eco-innovation strategies.

- **Companies with moderate experience** in green supply chains, on the other hand, may not prioritize training as highly. Instead, these firms should focus on enhancing their expertise and operational performance within the green supply chain, addressing inefficiencies, and optimizing their processes. More radical measures, such as adopting cutting-edge eco-technologies or overhauling existing workflows, can drive substantial improvements in their sustainability efforts.

2. Eco-Innovation and Decision-Making Eco-innovation is the integration of environmental considerations into management, design, and production processes. This approach encourages companies to reevaluate their decision-making frameworks and develop new products, services, and technologies that prioritize sustainability. Depending on a company's capabilities and resources, eco-innovation can manifest in various ways:

- **Incremental innovations** may involve making existing processes more efficient, such as reducing energy and material inputs or adopting less resource-intensive practices.
- **Radical innovations** might entail creating entirely new products or production methods, featuring characteristics like low energy consumption, unique designs, or identifiable environmental benefits.

These technological changes not only improve a company's environmental performance but also enhance its reputation in an increasingly eco-conscious market.

3. The Role of Education in Driving Change Building environmental awareness within an organization requires an emphasis on both formal education and continuous learning. For example:

- **Workshops and Seminars:** Interactive sessions can empower employees to understand sustainability principles and apply them to their roles.
- **On-the-Job Training:** Hands-on experiences enable employees to identify inefficiencies, experiment with new techniques, and adopt eco-innovative practices.
- **Collaborative Learning:** Partnering with experts or other organizations can provide fresh perspectives and innovative solutions tailored to specific challenges.

By investing in education and awareness initiatives, businesses can embed sustainability into their core values and operations.

4. The Impact of Technological Advancements Eco-innovation often involves leveraging technological advancements to reduce resource consumption and improve environmental performance. For example, companies can adopt innovative production processes that minimize energy usage, generate less waste, and optimize resource efficiency. Even seemingly small changes—such as introducing improved grinding processes or streamlining workflows—can contribute significantly to sustainability goals when scaled across an organization.

5. Empowering a Sustainable Future Through Knowledge Ultimately, education and awareness empower businesses to make informed decisions, adopt innovative practices, and champion sustainability. By equipping managers and employees with the knowledge and tools to prioritize eco-innovation, organizations can achieve meaningful environmental and economic benefits. A well-educated workforce not only drives internal change but also contributes to broader efforts to combat climate change and preserve the planet for future generations.

14

Government Policies and Regulations

Government policies and regulations play a crucial role in driving environmental sustainability. By leveraging their significant buying power and promoting eco-innovation, government bodies can set an example for businesses and the general public while accelerating the transition to greener practices.

1. Best Practices for Green IT Purchasing Policies For government organizations aiming to adopt green IT purchasing policies in Information and Communication Technology (ICT), the following five best practices have been identified:

- **Influencing Manufacturers and Purchasers:** Governments can use their purchasing power to demand greener technologies, encouraging manufacturers to prioritize eco-innovation.
- **Comprehensive Impact Assessment:** Reviewing and addressing the ICT-related environmental impact of the entire organization ensures alignment with sustainability goals.
- **Balancing Objectives:** Policies should also consider other organizational goals, such as usability, functionality, local supply chains, and product stewardship.

GOVERNMENT POLICIES AND REGULATIONS

- **Encouraging Innovation:** Governments should be open to adopting alternative and innovative methods that meet organizational needs while reducing environmental impact.
- **Raising Awareness:** Educating suppliers and employees on green IT principles fosters a culture of sustainability and shared responsibility.

Through these measures, governments can effectively reduce their own emissions while inspiring similar initiatives in the private sector.

2. Stimulating Innovation in Public and Private Sectors
Governments have the power to lead by example. By adopting sustainable practices in their own operations, they can encourage businesses and individuals to follow suit. For example, the effective use of ICT by governments can simultaneously reduce emissions and stimulate innovation in the public and private sectors. This dual impact underscores the importance of government-led initiatives in driving systemic change.

3. Economic and Environmental Impact of Green Procurement Worldwide, government purchasing accounts for approximately 12% of their GDP, equating to 2% of global GDP. This immense influence makes governmental procurement policies a powerful tool for promoting eco-innovative products and services. By mandating the use of eco-label-certified goods—such as Energy Star or EcoQLabel products—governments can significantly reduce energy consumption, material use, and carbon footprints.

The UK's Department for Environment, Food, and Rural Affairs (DEFRA) has demonstrated notable success in expanding the market for sustainable products. Beyond promoting eco-labeled goods, DEFRA has also supported the adoption of "freely available and open standards." Standards-based purchasing ensures consistency, scalability, and environmental impact reduction across products and services.

4. **Expanding the Reach of Eco-Innovation** The broader acceptance of eco-innovative goods through targeted government policies and regulations has the potential for profound global impact. Regulatory frameworks that prioritize sustainability can drive advancements in clean technology and encourage manufacturers to integrate environmental considerations into their design and production processes. Furthermore, the ripple effect of such policies can extend to international markets, fostering a global culture of sustainability.

5. **Building a Sustainable Future Through Policy Leadership** Government policies are instrumental in shaping a sustainable future. By adopting green procurement practices, promoting eco-innovative technologies, and encouraging private sector alignment, governments can create a lasting positive impact. Policymaking that addresses environmental challenges not only protects the planet but also spurs economic growth, innovation, and public trust.

Conclusion

Society's growing awareness of the challenges posed by the current economic model has ignited a global call for change. Technology, with its transformative potential, has opened new pathways to address these challenges. However, it raises an essential question: can the benefits of new technologies be overstated or misunderstood? And more importantly, to what extent can eco-innovations provide a comprehensive solution for sustainable development?

1. The Role of Policy in Driving Change While technology offers powerful tools for addressing environmental issues, it is not the sole solution. Based on the findings of this study, technological advancements do not inherently reveal the root causes of environmental degradation. Instead, they must be guided by robust environmental policies to ensure their effective application.

Environmental policy emerges as the cornerstone of sustainable development. Governments must enact and enforce stringent environmental regulations and standards across all sectors. By ensuring compliance and holding industries accountable, states can create a framework that encourages both innovation and responsibility. Policy-driven action provides the necessary foundation for eco-innovations to thrive and address complex environmental challenges.

2. Technology's Transformative Capabilities The ability of technology to uncover hidden environmental problems has grown exponentially, earning the past decade the title of "technology's decade." Advancements in monitoring tools and data analysis have illuminated issues that were previously unknown, unnoticed, or ignored. This capability not only facilitates the transition to a sustainable economy but also equips society with the knowledge to act decisively.

For instance, technology enables the monitoring of pollution contributions from various sectors, providing valuable insights into their environmental impact. Such data empowers policymakers, businesses, and communities to implement targeted solutions. However, production activities often create environmental problems that are not immediately visible or accounted for in pricing structures. These issues lead to long-term costs that must be addressed proactively.

3. The Path Forward: A Synergy of Technology and Policy
The intersection of technology and policy holds the key to a sustainable future. While technology can provide the tools to address environmental challenges, policy sets the direction and ensures accountability. By aligning these forces, society can drive meaningful progress toward a low-carbon economy, resource efficiency, and ecological preservation.

The solutions outlined in this study highlight the urgency of integrating eco-innovations with comprehensive environmental policies. Together, these elements can help create a world where sustainability is not just an aspiration but a reality.

4. A Call to Action The journey toward sustainability requires collective effort. As individuals, businesses, and governments, we must embrace our shared responsibility to protect the planet. By fostering innovation, implementing effective policies, and cultivating environmental awareness, we can leave a legacy of resilience and stewardship for future generations.

Technology alone cannot solve the challenges we face, but when guided by informed and intentional policies, it becomes a powerful force for change. The future of sustainable development lies in our ability to harness this synergy—transforming awareness into action, innovation into impact, and challenges into opportunities.

Enjoyed This Book? Let Others Know!

If this book has blessed, encouraged, or challenged you in any way, I'd love to hear about it! Your review not only helps others discover this message but also encourages me to keep writing.

Would you take a moment to share your thoughts? A few sentences on what stood out to you can make a big difference.

You can leave a review on Amazon, Goodreads, or wherever you purchased this book. Thank you for being part of this journey!

www.ingramcontent.com/pod-product-compliance
Lightning Source LLC
LaVergne TN
LVHW092100060526
838201LV00047B/1488